GUIDES TO EVERYTHING

GET OUT OF
D£BT
AND STAY OUT

By Jill Papworth

ISBN 978-1-84678-002-8

Copyright 2006, Quick123 Limited

Quick123 Limited, PO Box 45092, London N4 2ZJ.

Website: www.quick123.co.uk

Customer service or additional copies can be sought at service@quick123.co.uk.

Letter to the Reader

Anyone can get into debt. It's not something that only happens to spendthrifts and people who recklessly borrow money they can't afford to pay back. It's not just for those who simply 'haven't got a head for money'.

More often than not, debt problems hit people who suffer an unexpected drop in income, often for reasons beyond their control. They include illness, bereavement or a relationship breakdown.

There's no point wasting time feeling guilty or ashamed about being in debt. The golden rule is to act as quickly as possible to tackle the problem.

Debt problems will not go away if you ignore them: they will simply get worse. You could end up in court, lose your possessions, find it difficult to get credit or even lose your home.

Don't bury your head in the sand or waste time panicking. You need to act now! Be confident in the fact that you can escape debt and you are not alone in the struggle to do so.

This handy guide will explain the steps you need to take to get out of debt, then how to keep your borrowing and spending under control so that you stay out.

A lot of free help is available from experts in the UK for anyone with debt and money worries. We'll tell you where to find that help.

It's clear you are serious about tackling your debt problems because you've taken the first step by buying this guide. So, you're already on the right track.

Stay cool, follow the guidance and you will be debt free.

Jill Papworth

Contents

·GUIDES TO EVERYTHING·

Quick123 Limited
PO Box 45092
London N4 2ZJ

Email: peterpurton@quick123.co.uk

Dear Quick123 reader

Thank you for buying this guide. We hope you enjoy reading it.

Our aim is to help you achieve the goals you set yourself, whether it's getting a better job, improving relationships or creating a better you. And to help you achieve that without costing you too much time, effort or money.

Because you, the reader, are at the centre of everything we do, we'd like to hear from you. Whether you have comments about this book, ideas for a new topic or issues in your life you feel we might be able to help with, send us an email or a letter.

If we take up any of your ideas to create a new title we'll make sure you get your own special copy.

We want to provide you with the kinds of guides you want to read. With your help, I'm sure we can.

Happy reading,

Peter Purton

Peter Purton
Quick123 Limited

How much is too much?

Be honest, when was the last time you paid for a major item - something like a TV, a washing machine or a holiday - with money you'd saved up in advance? Can you even remember the last time you did that?

Once, people only felt comfortable spending money that they had saved up. These days, most of us don't think twice about borrowing money on credit cards and taking out loans to buy things we want.

We buy major items like cars along with everyday purchases like clothes, petrol and even the weekly grocery shop. Nowadays, there's little or no stigma attached to using credit to buy what we want, when we want it.

The problem comes in knowing how to tell when your borrowing is getting out of hand and you may be incurring debts you'll have trouble paying back. When does manageable credit turn into unmanageable debt? How much debt is too much debt?

Government statistics show that the average personal debt per adult in the UK on unsecured lending is £6,730. Unsecured loans are all types of borrowings excluding mortgages and any loans that are 'secured' on your home.

Wise Words
If you are in a cycle of debt, you are not powerless, although you may feel it. You can take practical steps and do something about the situation (Credit Action)

Recent research also shows that some 3 million credit card holders owe more than £1,500 each on their cards. One in four families owes an average of nearly £2,500 on at least one card.

Owing several thousand pounds on credit cards and other loans is not bad in itself. It may not be a problem for people with sufficient income to pay back the money.

Did You Know... ❓
One in 10 credit card holders - that's 23 million consumers - finds it difficult to pay off the interest on their account each month and always has a balance outstanding
(Source: consumer research group, Mintel)

For others, however, it can be a huge and worrying debt. It all depends on the size of your income and how easily you can cope with the monthly credit repayments you have to make.

So how can you tell if your debts are too high? One useful guideline comes from the Consumer Credit Counselling Service (CCCS), a charity that provides free debt counselling. *(see page 50).*

TOP TIPS

The danger signs

There are plenty of signs that you may be on the slippery slope towards unmanageable debt. Try the following checklist.
Are you:

- spending more on bills and living expenses than you've got coming in each month?
- Juggling your bills each month because you can't afford to pay them all?
- Cutting back on necessities like food or heating to pay creditors?
- Usually left with no money at the end of the month?
- Using an increasing amount of income to pay off debt?
- Up to two months behind with some credit payments?
- Near the credit limit on your credit and store cards?

- Only making the minimum repayments on credit cards?
- Missing credit payments?
- Frequently borrowing money from family, friends or colleagues?
- Using credit to buy small items you used to buy with cash?
- Paying household bills with a credit card?
- Regularly overdrawn on your current account?
- Not sure of your level of debt or borrowing?

If you answered "yes" to three or more of these questions, you could be in financial difficulties or, at least, heading that way. So you need to act now.

If you already have debt problems, it is important to face up to the fact and act swiftly or things will simply get worse.

Did You Know... ?
Nearly half the people who take out credit in shops hadn't planned to do so before they left home

Test yourself: The CCCS suggestion is that you: add up all the money you have to pay out servicing 'unsecured credit' each month. That's every minimum payment you have to make on credit and store cards plus all your monthly loan repayments.

If the total comes to more than a fifth of your monthly take-home income, you are in the debt danger zone. You need to make cuts in your spending.

Did You Know... ❓
One in five people regularly avoids checking their bank balance because they are too scared to find out how much money they have (or don't have!), according to Lloyds TSB

Keeping debt under control

One way of avoiding debt problems in the first place is to take control of your borrowing. That may be spending on credit cards, taking loans or going overdrawn on your current account. Make sure you don't over commit yourself.

Before you decide to borrow or take credit in any form, stop. Ask yourself the following questions and be tough with the answers:

- Can you really afford to pay back the money you'll be borrowing on top of any other regular repayments you have to make each month? Don't borrow money you can't repay

- Do you really need to borrow now? For example, could you wait for the sales to start and then buy what you want more cheaply?

- Do you *really* need the item you are thinking of buying and is it *truly* a good deal?

Sales pitches, special offers and store card deals are all designed to get you to part with your money. If you take time to think about what's on offer, you may realise you can do without the item you were thinking of buying and the extra debt you'd have to incur to get it.

Wise Words
By shopping around and taking time to think through the consequences of entering into a credit agreement, you can help to avoid debt problems occurring in the first place
(Office of Fair Trading)

If you do decide to go ahead and borrow money, follow these simple government guidelines:

- Shop around for credit. The first offer you get may not be the best deal

- Check out the different credit options - credit cards, overdrafts, 'buy now, pay later' instant credit and catalogues - to see which suits you best

- Read the forms and make sure you understand the small print before you sign any credit agreement

- Find out exactly how much you'll pay back, including interest and charges. Watch out for other charges such as brokers' or arrangement fees. Is it good value?

- Compare the APRs (annual percentage rates). That's the easiest way to compare similar credit products. For example, APRs vary enormously between different credit cards. Usually, the lower the APR, the less you have to pay

- Look at the length of the loan, not just the monthly payment. The longer the loan period, the more interest you'll pay back

- Be aware that if you go for a 'secured loan' - that's where you have to use your home as security - and you don't manage to keep up the repayments, you could lose the roof over your head

If you feel your credit level is getting out of control and you are sliding into debt:

- **Don't** go on a card-fuelled spending spree to cheer yourself up! Stop using your cards and taking on any more credit until you have cleared your debts. If you are short on self-discipline, cut up your cards or give them to someone you trust to keep them locked away

- **Do** stop any regular transfers from your current account to your savings accounts - make debt repayment your priority for the time being

- **Do** take a long hard look at your finances and try to set yourself a spending limit for the next few months

- **Do** make simple cutbacks to save money. Make a list and stick to it when you shop. Cut down on luxuries like cigarettes and magazines and make a packed lunch to take to work rather than buying pricey sandwiches. Use cash wherever possible for smaller purchases - spending *real money* will help you resist extra impulse buys

- **Do** be tough with yourself. A few hard weeks without any luxuries at all may be better than six months of half-hearted cutbacks - and the quicker you pay off your debts the less interest you'll pay

- **Don't** waste time being angry with yourself about getting into debt. Debt can happen to anyone and you are not alone

- **Don't** panic. Whatever the cause, debts *can* get out of hand fast and make life miserable. But you can sort things out and get back on a better financial footing, provided you act now

- **Do** tell your partner, a family member or friend about your money worries. It really can be true that 'a problem shared is a problem halved'. People may sympathise if they know you are struggling and may come up with some practical suggestions you haven't thought of

- **Don't** feel you have to cope alone. If you can't see a way of spending less each month and paying off your debts, get some help. There are plenty of professionals *(see page 49)* who won't judge you or charge you anything for advice on how to clear your debts

Wise Words
Letting your partner know the entire situation can be very difficult but helpful. Otherwise, they may continue to spend as before. It could even lead to a breakdown in trust if they discover the true position for themselves
(Consumer Credit Counselling Service)

Eight
steps to
tackling your
debts

Good news - you are on the right track. You've faced up to the fact that your debt problems are not going to go away but will only get worse unless you act now to tackle them.

Whether you plan to do that alone or with the help of a debt counsellor, there are some basic steps you need to take to clear your debts.

1. Draw up a personal budget

Creating a budget will give you a clear picture of exactly where your money goes - how much money comes in each month or week, how much you spend when out and on what.

It's the first step to gaining control over your finances. A personal budget will help you see where you can cut back on unnecessary spending and how much you can realistically afford to offer your creditors in the way of regular debt repayments.

Creating a budget may take a bit of time but you don't need to be a maths guru to do it. *Simply follow the guide that starts on page 23.*

Did You Know... ❓
A husband and wife are not responsible for each other's debts unless they have both signed the credit/loan agreement (except for Council Tax) and you cannot inherit a dead person's debts

2. Make a list of your creditors and debts
You may need to check your credit agreements or ask your creditors to find out the balance

owing, the terms of repayment, the interest and penalties accruing and the arrears.

3. Contact all your creditors

- that's every company and person to whom you owe money - as soon as possible to explain your situation and try to come to some arrangement about repayments.

The earlier they know about your financial difficulties and understand that you are trying to do something about clearing your debts, the more sympathetic they're likely to be.

If you fail to tell your creditors there's a problem, they will continue to add the costs of phone calls and written reminders to the interest you're already paying. Your debts will get even bigger.

Send them an explanatory letter and enclose a copy of your personal budget plus a list of your creditors and debts so they have a clear picture of your situation. Offer to pay what you can.

You'll find a sample letter at the end of this section. You can find other useful examples of letters you can adapt at www.nationaldebtline.co.uk and at www.creditaction.org.uk.

Your creditors are unlikely to write off your debts but they may be willing to accept smaller repayments over a longer period of time. They may even agree to freeze any further interest charged on your outstanding debt. That way, you can repay the amount you borrowed without any extra being added on.

Wise Words

When you contact creditors, if the first person you speak to is unhelpful, ask to speak to somebody more senior who may be able to agree to what you want. Don't give up trying to reach an agreement even if creditors are difficult
(National Debtline)

Generally, creditors will prefer to know they'll be getting back at least some of the money they have lent you in regular repayments rather than having to take you to court. They might then risk ending up with less or even with nothing.

Wise Words

Keep going! Don't despair - clearing your debts can be a long process but the end result will be worthwhile and will put you back in control of your financial situation
(Credit Action)

Don't bluff. If you make a repayment offer, make sure you can stick to the plan and do what you have promised.

You should start making payments as soon as you have fixed a repayment plan. This will encourage creditors to know you mean business and accept your proposals. Where possible, set up direct debits or standing orders to help you stick to your side of the deal.

4. Tackle your priority debts first

Concentrate first on repaying the ones that could have the most serious consequences if left unpaid. Mortgage or rent arrears come top of the list, because you are in danger of losing the roof over your head if you fail to repay them.

The section starting on *page 31* explains the possible consequences of different types of debts and how to prioritise them.

5. Think twice about borrowing more money to pay off your debts. Always steer clear of the loan sharks and credit brokers in the classified ads, who are likely to saddle you with more debt than you had before.

Bringing all your debts together into one 'roll up' or 'consolidation' loan is not always a good solution. It can be expensive and can put your home at greater risk if the loan is secured on it.

The monthly instalments on a consolidation loan may be lower, but you will normally have to pay them for a lot longer than your present loans. This type of deal can end up costing you far more in the long run.

Bringing all your debts together may give you less chance of negotiating reduced payments with individual creditors. This will mean less flexibility and more to lose if you don't keep up your repayments.

So, before taking out a consolidation loan, do take advice from a professional debt counsellor to ensure that you are not simply increasing your overall debt.

See p. 49 for debt counsellor contact details.

6. Don't ignore any court summons you receive
Fill in the reply forms to court summons papers, attend hearings and let the court have all the facts. This information will be used to decide if you owe the money and what instalments you should pay.

7. Contact your creditors regularly
Answer all their letters, phone calls and e-mails. If you promise to get back to a creditor, make sure you do contact them before *they* have to contact *you* again.

8. Always keep records of correspondence
Make a note of every telephone conversation, with the date, time and name of the person you spoke to. Keep copies of all letters and e-mails.

On the following pages you will see a sample of a letter to creditors as recommended by **National Debtline**.

Did You Know...
Creditors are allowed to remind you if you miss repayments but they are not allowed to harass you by improper methods. If they do, tell your local trading standards or consumer protection department

**NATIONAL DEBTLINE
SAMPLE LETTER** to send to
creditors when offering a new repayment
schedule. Also include a copy of your personal
budget and a list of your creditors and debts.

Creditor's name and address:

Your address
Date

Dear Sir/Madam
Account No.
. . . .
. . . .
Since making the above agreement with
you, my/our circumstances have changed.

I/We cannot now afford the agreed monthly
payments because . . . .
*(explain here what the problems are, for example
if you have lost your job, separated from your
partner, or had an unexpected increase in
outgoings or drop in income).*

I/We enclose a personal budget sheet
which shows my/our total income from all
sources, and my/our total outgoings. As
you can see I/we have only £xxxx per
month left for my/our creditors.

The offers I/we have made to my/our creditors have been worked out on a *prorata* basis, and I/we have written to all my/our creditors asking them to accept reduced offers. In view of my/our circumstances, please would you agree to accept a reduced offer of £xxxxx per month. If interest or other charges are being added to the account, I/we would be grateful if you would freeze these so that all payments made will reduce what I/we owe you.

Should my/our circumstances improve I/we will contact you again.

I/we would be grateful if you would send a [paying-in book] [standing order form] *(choose the payment method you want)* to make it easier to pay.

Thank you for your assistance. I/we look forward to hearing from you as soon as possible.

Yours faithfully,

(Your signature with your name printed underneath)

How to work out a personal budget

It is vital to work out a personal budget so that you can see where your money is going. It will show how much you can realistically afford to offer to pay your creditors each month.

You will also need it to show to your creditors so that they have a clear picture of your financial situation. You'll find a specimen budget chart on *page 28*.

Your budget sheet needs to list absolutely all the regular income you receive from whatever source. It must also show every penny of the money you spend when out - and where it goes.

Under your income section, include figures for your net salary - that's your take-home pay after tax, National Insurance, pension contributions and any other deductions have been made. Also include any regular bonuses, tips and overtime pay that you know you can rely on getting.

Did You Know... ❓
There are very useful interactive budget calculators you can use to work out your personal budget online at: www.fsa.gov.uk/consumer; www.moneybasics.co.uk; www.bbc.co.uk/radio1/onelife/finance; **and** www.insolvencyhelpline.co.uk

If you get any other regular income that's not listed, include that under 'Other'. Don't include one-off lump sums you may receive such as an inheritance or prize money. Sudden windfalls like these should be treated as an unexpected bonus, not income that can be relied upon to fund regular outgoings.

Under your expenses section, make sure you include occasional outgoings like Christmas, birthdays, treats and holidays and don't forget to allow a realistic amount for irregular and often unexpected costs such as car maintenance, house decoration and repairs and furniture or white goods replacements.

You can choose to use either monthly or weekly figures when drawing up your budget, but don't mix the two.

TOP TIPS

- If you want to change weekly figures to monthly, multiply by 52 and then divide by 12.

- If you want to change monthly figures to weekly, multiply by 12 and then divide by 52.

- For annual payments such as road tax, your TV licence fee and Christmas presents, divide by 12 to get a monthly figure or by 52 to get a weekly figure.

If, apart from the obvious regular outgoings like your rent or mortgage and fuel bills, you really have no idea what your money gets spent on each week or month, you'll have to find out. Use a notebook and monitor your spending for a minimum of a week and ideally for a month.

Keep the notebook with you at all times and note down *everything* you spend, no matter how trivial the amount. You'll have to be rigorously honest. As well as major outlays - for example at the supermarket or petrol station - include small items such as newspapers, snacks and bus fares.

This exercise will give you the vital information you need to draw up your personal budget. As a bonus, you may find that carrying a spending diary around with you makes you spend less. It will make you think twice if you know you have to record each time you dip into your wallet.

Your household budget may differ from the one shown in our sample sheet. You may have extra expenses because of your particular circumstances, or there may be some expenses we have listed that you don't have. Remember it's your budget and you should include all your relevant figures.

If you use your personal budget to send as a financial statement to creditors, at the top put the date it was prepared. Also include your name and address and details of the number of adults and children in your household.

"Try and make your expenses less than your income, otherwise your debts will continue to grow. However, do be realistic. You may have to live on this budget for several years, so concentrate on reducing non-essentials rather than basics such as food and heating" (Credit Action)

You will need to revise and update it regularly to reflect any changes in your circumstances, income and expenditure. Any regular payments you subsequently agree to make to creditors will need adding in too.

YOUR PERSONAL BUDGET

Income weekly/monthly   £

Wages/salary (take-home pay)   _ _ _ _ _ _ _

Partner's wages/salary (take-home pay)   _ _ _ _ _ _ _

State benefits and/or tax credits   _ _ _ _ _ _ _

Pension   _ _ _ _ _ _ _

Child Benefit   _ _ _ _ _ _ _

Child maintenance paid to you   _ _ _ _ _ _ _

Rent or money from lodgers   _ _ _ _ _ _ _

Money from part-time jobs   _ _ _ _ _ _ _

Contributions from family members   _ _ _ _ _ _ _

Income from savings or investments   _ _ _ _ _ _ _
Any other income   _ _ _ _ _ _ _

_ _ _ _ _ _ _

TOTAL INCOME   _ _ _ _ _ _ _

Outgoings weekly/monthly   £
Mortgage/rent   _ _ _ _ _ _ _
Mortgage endowment policy   _ _ _ _ _ _ _
Second mortgage   _ _ _ _ _ _ _
Council Tax   _ _ _ _ _ _ _
Water   _ _ _ _ _ _ _
Maintenance paid by you   _ _ _ _ _ _ _
Electricity   _ _ _ _ _ _ _
Gas   _ _ _ _ _ _ _
Other fuel   _ _ _ _ _ _ _

Service charges/ground rent	_ _ _ _ _ _ _ _
Magistrates' court fines	_ _ _ _ _ _ _ _
Vehicle finance/hire purchase	_ _ _ _ _ _ _ _
Road tax and MOT	_ _ _ _ _ _ _ _
Home insurance	_ _ _ _ _ _ _ _
Car insurance	_ _ _ _ _ _ _ _
Food and housekeeping	_ _ _ _ _ _ _ _
School meals/meals at work	_ _ _ _ _ _ _ _
Clothing and shoes	_ _ _ _ _ _ _ _
Petrol/diesel	_ _ _ _ _ _ _ _
Travel fares	_ _ _ _ _ _ _ _
Childcare costs	_ _ _ _ _ _ _ _
Prescriptions/dentist/optician	_ _ _ _ _ _ _ _
School costs	_ _ _ _ _ _ _ _
TV Licence	_ _ _ _ _ _ _ _
Rentals - TV, video, DVD	_ _ _ _ _ _ _ _
Telephone/mobile phone	_ _ _ _ _ _ _ _
Life insurance	_ _ _ _ _ _ _ _
Investment/pension contributions	_ _ _ _ _ _ _ _
Christmas/birthdays	_ _ _ _ _ _ _ _
Holidays	_ _ _ _ _ _ _ _
Sports and leisure	_ _ _ _ _ _ _ _
Cigarettes/alcohol	_ _ _ _ _ _ _ _
Hairdresser	_ _ _ _ _ _ _ _
Dry cleaning	_ _ _ _ _ _ _ _
Other	_ _ _ _ _ _ _ _
	_ _ _ _ _ _ _ _
TOTAL	_ _ _ _ _ _ _ _

Once you have filled in your budget sheet, check it through. Creditors may challenge amounts you spend on food and clothing for example. You will need to consider whether the amounts you spend are reasonable for your size of household and, if not, whether you can reduce them to a more realistic level.

Creditors may also question whether other costs such as leisure, sport and holiday costs and cigarettes are necessary. You'll need to be able to justify non-essential costs or think of ways of cutting back on them.

It's now crunch time. Deduct your total outgoings from your total income figure and see what's left. The money left over is what you can afford to spread between your creditors in debt repayments.

If there is no money over, meaning that your outgoings are higher than your income, you are in serious trouble because your debts will continue to get bigger. If this is the case, you need to find ways to increase your income or reduce your outgoings - ideally, both.

Prioritise your debts

If you've built up a variety of different debts, you may be confused and unsure about which ones to concentrate on paying off first. The key is to prioritise your debts in order of their scariness.

Some types of debts have more serious consequences than others if you leave them unpaid. That means that you should deal with them first. The size of each debt or how long you've had it is irrelevant.

What matters is the type of action that different creditors are allowed to take by law in order to get their money back.

If non-payment of a debt could result in:

• You going to prison

• Losing your home through repossession or eviction

• Having essential services like your gas or electricity cut off

• Having furniture taken from your home by bailiffs then it is a **priority debt**.

Did You Know...

Creditors can take action on some priority debts without going to court first. For example, gas and electricity companies can disconnect you. There does not need to be a court order before bailiffs can be used for VAT and income tax debts

---

It is important that you use the money you have available for creditors to settle these debts first before you make any offers of payment on 'secondary debts'. Secondary debts are the ones that do not carry the same potentially serious consequences.

> **Wise Words** ❗
> **Your other priority creditors can take action against you only after court action. But don't panic. You will always be given warning and, provided you act quickly, you should be able to stop these things happening** (National Debtline)

1. Main types of priority debt

Mortgage arrears. If you get behind with your mortgage payments and build up arrears you don't pay off, you could lose your home. So if you can't meet your mortgage repayments or you are worried you might fall behind in future, contact your mortgage lender as soon as possible.

Lenders have procedures for tackling payment difficulties and they will try to help. Most lenders are regulated by the FSA (Financial Services Authority), whose rules say that lenders must treat you fairly and agree a payment plan that is practical for you, given your circumstances.

There are also clear rules covering what the lender must do if it intends to repossess your home. You can get more details by going to www.fsa.gov.uk/consumer.

If you are having difficulty paying your mortgage because you've lost your job or you are too ill to work, check whether you've got 'mortgage payment protection insurance' which will cover your payments in such circumstances. If so, contact your insurer about making a claim.

If you are claiming certain state benefits - income support, pension credit or income-based job seeker's allowance - you may be able to get help with some of the interest payments on your mortgage from the Government's department of work and pensions (DWP). Find out more from your nearest Jobcentre Plus.

It is important that you pay as much as you can manage of your monthly mortgage repayments. Keeping up regular payments, even if they vary, shows that you are committed and will encourage your lender to treat you sympathetically.

2. Secondary mortgage/'secured' loans

A second mortgage is a separate loan that is secured on your home. You should check all your loan agreements to see if they are 'unsecured' or 'secured' on your home. If they are secured loans and you can't pay your monthly instalments, lenders can ask the court for possession of your home to be sold off to pay off your debt. So you could lose your home.

3. Rent arrears

If you fail to pay your rent, then landlords can take you to court and apply to have you evicted from your home (remember, tenants cannot be evicted without a court order). So, it is vital you contact your landlord and explain your situation as soon as you have difficulty paying your rent.

There are several different types of tenancy and each type gives you different legal rights. Your right to stay in your home depends on the type of tenancy you have so it is essential for you to find out.

If you are not sure, get help by contacting your local Citizens Advice Bureau or Shelter's free housing advice helpline on 0808 800 4444. You can also call the National Debtline on 0808 808 4000.

4. Council Tax

If you don't pay your council tax, the council can ask the magistrates' court to make a 'liability order' for the full amount that they say you owe.

If you don't pay this, the council is able to get the money from you using one of several drastic methods.

They can order your employer to take a fixed amount from your wages or, if you don't work, arrange deductions from your state benefits. They can ask bailiffs to visit your home and take goods that may be sold to pay your arrears.

Did You Know... ❓
Since the Water Act 1999, water companies can no longer disconnect your supply if you are in arrears

If you still don't pay, they can ultimately apply for you to be sent to prison. So, if at any point you find you can't pay your full monthly instalment, don't just stop paying. Pay what you can afford and contact your council to try to come to an arrangement.

5. TV Licence

If you don't have a current licence you can be fined in the magistrates' court. This can lead to bailiffs calling or even to imprisonment if you don't pay the fine.

There is a 50% reduction in the price of a licence if you or someone you live with is registered blind, and a licence is free if you are 75 or over. There are a variety of ways to pay your licence fee. For details, see www.tvlicensing.co.uk.

6. Gas or electricity

If you don't pay your fuel bills, gas and electricity companies can cut off your supply in a few weeks and they don't need a court order to do so. So contact your suppliers as soon as you know you are going to have trouble paying your bills and make a payment arrangement.

7. Magistrates' court fines

If a magistrates' court orders you to pay a fine, you can ultimately be sent to prison if you don't pay it.

Note that, if you have been sued for a credit debt such as a loan or outstanding credit card bill, the case is heard in the county court and you cannot be sent to prison for failure to pay. That is why that type of debt is secondary and not priority.

8. Maintenance orders

Whether you fail to pay maintenance that has been ordered by the court as part of a separation or divorce process, or by the Child Support Agency, the money you owe can be taken from your wages or through sale of goods seized from your home by bailiffs.

At worst you can be sent to prison for failure to pay. So, if you are in arrears with maintenance, contact the court or CSA straight away (whichever is relevant), and explain the problem.

9. Hire purchase

If you fail to keep up repayments on a hire purchase agreement, the creditor can repossess the goods.

If you've paid less than a third of the total owed under the agreement, the goods can be repossessed even without a court order. This is serious if the goods in question are an essential requirement for you; for example, a car needed for work.

10. Income tax, National Insurance and VAT arrears

Failure to pay money you owe to HM Revenue & Customs can lead to bailiffs seizing your possessions, to bankruptcy and, ultimately, to imprisonment.

National Debtline publishes a free fact sheet: 'How to Deal with Business debts'. This is available if you call 0808 808 4000; you can also download it at www.nationaldebtline.co.uk

Any other type of debt, including outstanding credit card bills, loans, overdrafts and catalogue bills, can be treated as a secondary debt. These debts do not carry the same legal sanctions as priority debts, which should be settled first.

It is still important to pay off secondary debts. You may find it hard to get credit in the future if you stall credit repayments for too long.

Maximise your income: make your money go further

Showing creditors your personal budget sheet and asking them to accept your offers of payment is not the end of the story. They will want reassurance that you have done everything you can to minimize your expenditure and to maximize your income.

Check that you are claiming all the state benefits and tax credits you can. Lots of people are in debt simply because they don't receive all the money they are entitled to. Millions of pounds in allowances and benefits go unclaimed every year. It's not easy getting your head around the complex state benefits system, but the main things you need to know are outlined below.

Benefits can broadly be divided into two main types. Means-tested benefits are paid only if you have limited income and capital (e.g., savings). This means there is an investigation of your 'means' before these benefits are paid to you.

Non-means-tested benefits don't depend on your income and savings. You qualify if you satisfy certain basic conditions. These include being available for work, disabled, pregnant or a parent.

There are two types of non-means-tested benefits. Contributory benefits are funded by the National Insurance (NI) contributions you pay while you are in work. You can only get them if you have made sufficient contributions in the past. Non-contributory benefits are paid from taxation and do not depend on your NI contributions.

You can get details and descriptions of and leaflets on all the different kinds of benefits on the Department for Work and Pensions website at www.dwp.gov.uk or call the public enquiry line on 020 7712 2171. Leaflets are also available at your local Jobcentre or social security office.

Visiting the DWP website should give you a good idea of what benefits you might be entitled to. But seek advice if you are unsure.

Benefits specialists at your local Citizens Advice Bureau or other local advice centre will help you check that you are claiming all the correct benefits.

To apply for benefits, start by contacting your local Jobcentre or social security office - the number will be in the phonebook or you can find your nearest office at www.jobcentreplus.gov.uk.

Some benefits and tax credits to consider are:

- Job Seeker's Allowance - if you are unemployed or have been made redundant

- Income Support - if you are on a low income but not able to sign on for work for particular reasons, such as being ill or caring for someone

- Pension Credit - if you are 60 and over and are on a low income. For an application form, call 0800 99 1234

- Working Tax Credit - if you are working but on a low income, this can be paid on top of your wages

- Child Tax Credit - if you are on a low income and have responsibility for children under 16, or 19 if in full time education

For more information on tax credits visit www.hmrc.gov.uk or call the tax credits helpline on 0845 300 3900

- Child Benefit - if you have children, whatever your income, you should already be getting this non-means-tested benefit. If you are not, call the enquiry line on 0845 302 1444

- Incapacity or Disablement Benefits - if you are disabled, you or your carer can get free telephone advice on benefits on 0800 882 200

- Housing Benefit - if you are on a low income and paying rent. The benefit is paid by your local council and you don't have to be getting any other benefits to claim it

- Council Tax Benefit - if you are on a low income and have to pay council tax. Paid by your local council, you don't have to be getting any other benefits to qualify. It doesn't matter if you already get a discount on your council tax; for example if you live alone

- Education Maintenance Allowance - if you are on a low income and you have children aged 16 plus who are staying on at school or college, they may qualify for this. Find out more at www.direct.gov.uk/ema or ring the EMA helpline on 0808 101 6219

Other ways of boosting your income

- Could you increase your overtime earnings?

- What about getting a second job in the evenings or at weekends?

- Make sure you are not paying too much tax. Check with your local tax office to make sure that you have the right tax code, particularly if your circumstances have changed. You may be entitled to a rebate. Some employees can claim tax relief on work-related expenses. You can get a higher tax allowance if you are registered blind, were widowed before 5 April 2000 or if you are over 65

- If you have children from a former relationship, are you claiming any or enough maintenance from your former partner? Find out more by calling the Child Support Agency enquiry line on 0845 7133 133

- If you have grown-up children or other relatives or friends living with you, make sure they are paying enough towards the housekeeping expenses

- If you've got a spare room in your home, think about taking in a lodger. Under the Rent-a-Room scheme, you can receive rent of up to £4,250 a year per household completely free of tax if you let one or more furnished rooms in your house - for details contact your nearest tax office

- If you are thinking of making an income from lodgers, do check first how it could affect any benefits you get and make sure you have permission from your landlord or mortgage lender to rent out rooms

Did You Know...

If you are claiming Income Support or Job Seeker's Allowance there may be work that you can do without it affecting your benefit, such as fostering. You may be able to work as a child minder and still claim Income Support. Some of your earnings are ignored and you are not held to be working full time

The rules are different if you are on Job Seeker's Allowance. Check with the Department for Work and Pensions

(National Debtline)

- Look at the other side of your personal budget sheet and see if there are any obvious ways of cutting your expenditure. Go through every item and ask yourself:

1. Do I really need this?

2. Can I reduce the amount I spend on it?

3. Can I replace it with a cheaper alternative? Whatever the cause and extent of your debt problem, don't feel you have to cope alone. There are lots of sources of free, confidential, expert advice available to you.

Wise Words
Don't be too proud to ask for help. Struggling on alone is unlikely to provide the best answer to your problems

Where to get free help

Several organisations put you in touch with an impartial debt counsellor who will help you to identify ways of reducing your spending and maximising your income. They will help you to prioritise your debts and negotiate affordable and realistic debt repayment plans with your creditors.

You can opt to use as little or as much of this help as you wish. You might, for example, be happy to take the DIY approach and simply get some advice on how to help yourself out of debt. Alternatively, a specialist debt counsellor can help you through it.

You can pick and choose from the list of help resources listed below.

The Office of Fair Trading
The OFT is running a campaign to help people

deal with their debt problems. You can download a guide, 'In Debt? Help Yourself Out!', and get tips for sorting out your debts at www.oft.gov.uk

Citizens Advice Bureaux

CABs give free, impartial, confidential and face-to-face advice on debt from over 3,000 outlets around the UK.

Advisers will also talk about your benefit entitlements and legal rights and will represent you in court if necessary. Volunteer advisers will pass complex financial cases to specialist, full-time money advice workers.

Details of your nearest bureau can be found in the phonebook or visit www.citizensadvice.org.uk

Local authority money advice centres

See local phonebook. These centres work on similar lines to CABs.

Consumer Credit Counselling Service (CCCS)

A charity offering a free, confidential advice service for people in debt through its free national telephone service and eight centres. It provides counselling on personal budgeting, advice on the wise use of credit and, where appropriate, on managing achievable plans to repay debts.

Freephone helpline 0800 138 1111 open 8am to 8pm, Monday to Friday. Website: www.cccs.co.uk

National Debtline

A national telephone helpline that provides free confidential and independent advice on how to tackle debt problems.

The service provides self-help advice to its callers followed up with self-help packs and fact sheets sent free to their homes (also downloadable from its website). Where appropriate, it can also assist callers in setting up debt management plans.

Freephone 0808 808 4000 open 9am to 9pm, Monday to Friday and 9.30am-1pm Saturday. Website: www.nationaldebtline.co.uk

Credit Action

A national money education charity committed to

helping people manage their money better. It offers a range of resources, including debt advice guides, which can be downloaded from its website.

People in need of debt counselling are advised to contact the Consumer Credit Counselling Service (see above) with whom Credit Action works closely. Website: www.creditaction.org.uk

AdviceUK

A trade association for over 1,000 information and advice centres, about 300 of which provide debt advice. To find your nearest advice centre, call AdviceUK on 020 7407 4070 or visit www.adviceuk.org.uk or look in the Yellow Pages under 'counselling and advice'.

For advice centres in Northern Ireland, contact AdviceNI on 028 9064 5919 or visit www.adviceni.net

Money Basics

www.moneybasics.co.uk has useful money management information and tips.

Debt Management Companies

The wealth of free debt counselling services available means there is really no need for you to resort to using one of the debt management companies (DMCs) operating in the UK. These are private firms that offer fee-charging services to people with multiple debt problems.

The firms advertise in newspapers and on daytime television using slogans such as "Write off all your debts!" or "Make a fresh start!". They will claim to bring all your loans, credit and store card liabilities and other debts into one 'easy to pay' reduced monthly payment.

DMCs charge a fee for providing debt advice and rescheduling payments. They will also negotiate with creditors and distribute the monthly payments to creditors on a customer's behalf.

While they may well cut your monthly debt repayments, you normally end up paying out a lot more in the long run. You make the repayments for longer and pay an extra interest charge on top.

If, however, you do consider using the services of a DMC, before you sign up make sure you understand exactly what you are signing up to.

The Office of Fair Trading suggests that you:

• check that the contract clearly explains the nature and cost of the service being offered

• make sure that details of the total cost to you, the amount to be repaid and the duration of the contract are set out clearly

• understand all the possible consequences of entering it: how it may affect your credit rating and ability to get credit

• check that the circumstances in which you may withdraw from the contract and receive a refund are in the terms and conditions of the contract

And finally

If there is one thing I would like you to remember after reading this, it is that, however worried and frightened you feel right now about your debts, there is light at the end of the tunnel.

If you act now, take the steps suggested in this guide and take advantage of the wealth of free help available, you can and will be free of debt at some point in the future.

Imagine how great you'll feel then!

Further

• •

Updates to this guide can be found at:
www.quick123.co.uk/debt

Money for Life:
Everyone's Guide to Financial Freedom
by Alvin Hall.
Published by Coronet Books.
ISBN 034079321X

What Not to Spend
by Alvin Hall.
Published by Hodder & Stoughton.
ISBN 0340836024

Get Your Finances Sorted
by Mark Dalton and Geoffrey Dalton.
Published by Harper Collins.
ISBN 0722537468

reading

••••••••••••••••••••••••••••••

**The Complete Cheapskate:
How to Get Out of Debt, Stay Out
and Break Free From Money
Worries Forever**
by Mary Hunt.
Published by St Martin's Griffin.
ISBN 0312316046

**How To Get Out of Debt,
Stay Out of Debt & Live Prosperously**
by Jerrold Mundis.
Published by Bantam Books.
ISBN 0553283960